For my love, Abel.
Thank you for being such a loving and supportive father and partner.
I am so grateful for you.

Little Healers
Relax to Sleep

Written by
Becky Payne

Illustrated by
Moran Reudor

Today was
a wonderful day.
What did you
do today?

It is time to let
go of the day,
relax and get
ready to sleep.

Take a big breath in.
Take a big breath out.
As you breathe out,
relax your body.

Breathe in.
Breathe out.
Relax.

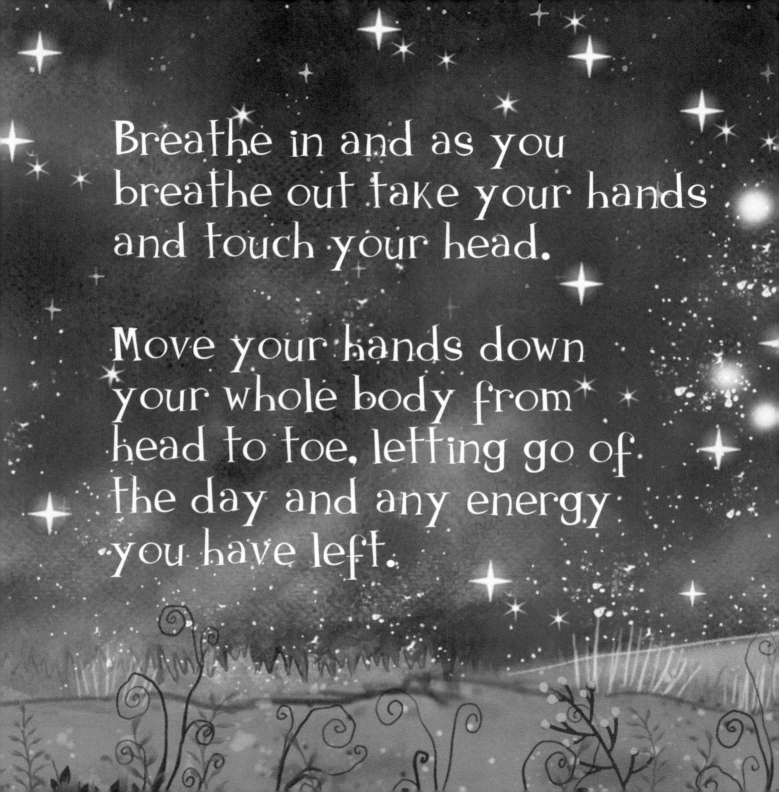

Breathe in and as you breathe out take your hands and touch your head.

Move your hands down your whole body from head to toe, letting go of the day and any energy you have left.

Breathe in. Breathe out
and move your hands from
your head all the way down
your body to your toes.
Release energy.

One more time.
Big breath in and
a big breath out
as you move
your hands
from your
head to your toes.

You are peaceful and safe
as you breathe in,
breathe out and relax.

As you go to bed tonight
know that you are protected,
safe and you are loved!

Sweet dreams little healer.

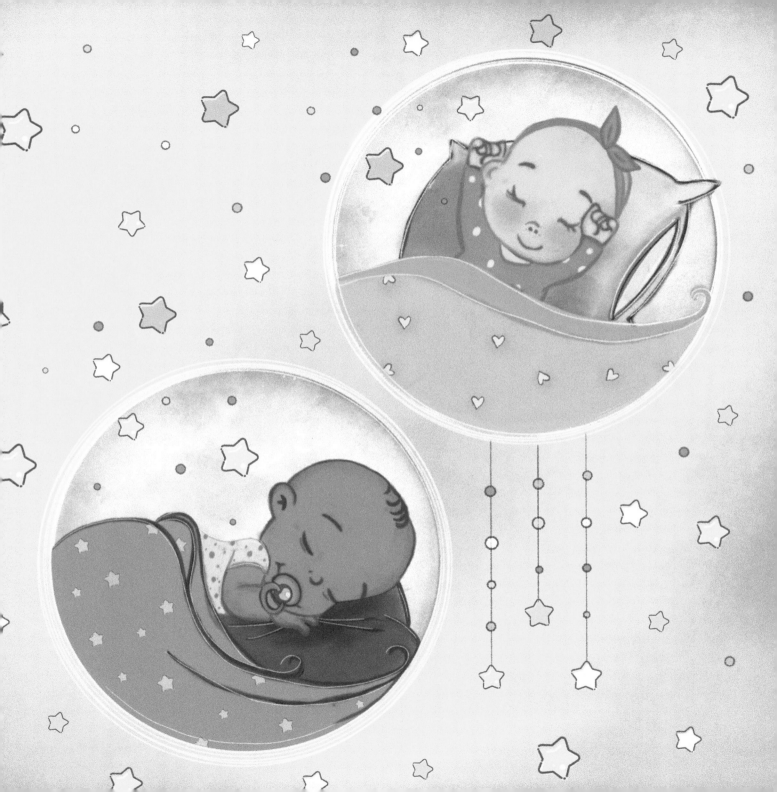

CPSIA information can be obtained
at www.ICGtesting.com
Printed in the USA
JSHW071201240523
42046JS00002B/88

9 781737 832225